# thai

simple and delicious easy-to-make recipes

Lesley Mackley

This is a Parragon Publishing Book

This edition published in 2004

Parragon Publishing
Queen Street House
4 Queen Street
Bath, BA1 1HE, UK

ISBN: 1-40543-645-X

Printed in China

Produced by
THE BRIDGEWATER BOOK COMPANY LTD

Photographer: Simon Punter
Home Economist: Ricky Turner

Cover Photography: Calvey Taylor-Haw
Home Economist: Ruth Pollock

## NOTES FOR THE READER

- This book uses both imperial, metric, and cup measurements. Follow the same units of measurement throughout; do not mix imperial and metric.

- All spoon measurements are level: teaspoons are assumed to be 5 ml, and tablespoons are assumed to be 15 ml.

- Unless otherwise stated, milk is assumed to be whole milk, eggs and individual vegetables such as potatoes are medium, and pepper is freshly ground black pepper.

- Recipes using raw or very lightly cooked eggs should be avoided by infants, the elderly, pregnant women, convalescents, and anyone suffering from an illness.

- The times given are an approximate guide only. Preparation times differ according to the techniques used by different people and the cooking times may also vary from those given. Optional ingredients, variations, or serving suggestions have not been included in the calculations.

# contents

# introduction

Thai cooking has become increasingly popular in the last few years, and the main ingredients, which not so long ago could be found only in specialist shops, have now become widely available.

Chilies are an essential ingredient in many dishes, and if you are not used to them, add them with caution. However, the use of coconut milk and fragrant herbs and spices has a cooling effect on the heat of the chilies. It should not be difficult to find the other ingredients used in these recipes, but if, for instance, fresh lemongrass or lime leaves are unavailable, it will not affect the recipe if dried ones are used. Lemongrass is also available in a purée. If you find fresh lime leaves and lemongrass, it is worth stocking up, because they freeze very well. Fish sauce is the Thai equivalent to soy sauce and is used as a seasoning instead of salt. It gives a distinctive flavor to many Thai dishes, but if it is difficult to find, use soy sauce instead.

aromatic chicken & vegetable soup
page 12

tiger shrimp skewers
page 32

Many dishes in this book are suitable for vegetarians, and you can substitute soy sauce for fish sauce when the latter occurs in an otherwise vegetarian recipe. Thai cooking can be addictive, and once you are familiar with the ingredients and able to balance different flavors, you will enjoy adapting the recipes to your own taste.

## Key to Recipes

easy

Recipes are graded as follows:
1 spoon = easy;
2 spoons = very easy;
3 spoons = extremely easy.

serves 4

Recipes generally serve four people. Simply halve the ingredients to serve two, taking care not to mix metric and imperial measurements.

15 minutes

Preparation time. Where marinating or soaking are involved, these times have been added on separately: eg, 15 minutes + 30 minutes to marinate.

40 minutes

Cooking time. Cooking times do not include the cooking of side dishes or accompaniments served with the main dishes.

stir-fried chicken with thai basil
page 50

tropical fruit in lemongrass syrup
page 86

In Thailand, soups usually stay on the table throughout the meal. They can serve as a sauce for rice or dishes that have no sauce of their own. Some soups, such as Hot & Sour Fish Soup, are very light and can be served as a first course, whereas others are more substantial and may be served as a light lunch or supper dish. Finger food, particularly when sold on the street, is very popular in Thailand. Snacks such as Spring Rolls, Chicken Satay, or Hot Chili Relish with Crudités (Nam Prik) can be served as an appetizer or as party food with drinks.

soups, appetizers
& snacks

# chicken & coconut milk soup

extremely easy

serves 4

10 minutes

15 minutes

### ingredients

1¾ cups canned coconut milk
scant 2¼ cups chicken bouillon
6 thin slices fresh galangal
2 stalks fresh lemongrass, bruised
4 fresh kaffir lime leaves
8 oz/225 g chicken breast fillets,
  cut into strips

2 red chilies, seeded and sliced finely
4 scallions, sliced finely
4 tbsp fish sauce
2 tbsp lime juice
2 tbsp chopped fresh cilantro

Place the coconut milk, chicken bouillon, galangal, lemongrass, and lime leaves
in a large pan and bring to a boil.

Add the chicken, then reduce the heat and simmer, uncovered, for 10 minutes,
or until the chicken is cooked.

Add the chilies and scallions and simmer for 3 more minutes.

Stir in the fish sauce, lime juice, and cilantro and serve immediately,
in warmed bowls.

# hot & sour shrimp soup

very easy    serves 4–6

30 minutes    30 minutes

## ingredients

1 lb 2 oz/500 g large raw shrimp, in shells
1 cup oyster mushrooms, sliced thinly
2 tsp light soy sauce
1 tsp white sugar
4 scallions, sliced finely
2 tsp fish sauce
2 tbsp chopped fresh cilantro

BOUILLON
1 lb/450 g white fish bones
8 cups water
2 stalks of fresh lemongrass, chopped finely
2–4 small dried red chilies
4 fresh or dried kaffir lime leaves
1 inch/2.5 cm fresh gingerroot, peeled
2 slices of fresh or dried galangal

To make the bouillon, peel the shrimp and place the shells in a large saucepan with the fish bones, water, lemongrass, chilies, lime leaves, gingerroot, and galangal. Bring to the boil, reduce the heat and simmer, covered, for 20 minutes.

Strain the bouillon into another large pan. Add the shrimp, mushrooms, soy sauce, sugar, and scallions. Bring back to the boil, then reduce the heat and simmer for 3 minutes, or until the shrimp are cooked. Add the fish sauce and cilantro, cook for 1 more minute, then serve immediately.

# aromatic chicken & vegetable soup

very easy    serves 4

15 minutes   30 minutes

## ingredients

handful of fresh cilantro
4 cups chicken bouillon
1 stalk fresh lemongrass, bruised
1 small fresh red chili
grated zest and juice of ½ lime
salt and pepper

8 oz/225 g chicken breast fillet, diced
1 cup snow peas, cut into thin
   diagonal strips
1 carrot, shaved into ribbons
3½ oz/100 g baby corn, sliced thinly
4 scallions, sliced thinly

Strip the cilantro leaves from the stalks. Reserve the leaves and place the stalks in a large pan with the bouillon, lemongrass, chili, and lime zest. Bring to a boil, then reduce the heat and simmer, covered, for 15 minutes.

Strain the bouillon into another pan. Add the lime juice, and salt and pepper to taste.

Add the chicken to the bouillon. Bring to a boil, then reduce the heat and simmer for 5 minutes. Add the snow peas, carrot, and corn and simmer for about 2 minutes, or until the vegetables are tender and the chicken is cooked.

Coarsely chop the cilantro leaves and stir into the soup with the scallions. Serve immediately.

# spring rolls

easy    makes 30

20 minutes    15 minutes
(food cooked
in batches)

## ingredients

1 tbsp corn oil

2¼ cups lean ground pork

1 garlic clove, crushed

1 red chili, seeded and chopped finely

4 oz/115 g cooked shrimp, shelled,
  and chopped

2 scallions, chopped finely

1 inch/2.5 cm piece gingerroot,
  grated finely

2 tbsp chopped fresh cilantro

2 tsp fish sauce

30 spring roll wrappers

oil, for deep frying

sweet chili sauce, to serve

Heat the oil in a skillet. Add the pork, garlic, and chili and cook, stirring, until the pork is browned.

Add the shrimp, scallions, ginger, cilantro, and fish sauce. Cook, stirring, until heated through. Remove from the heat and set aside to cool.

Prepare the spring roll wrappers as directed on the package.

Place a spoonful of the pork mixture down the middle of each spring roll sheet, leaving a space at the top and bottom and down the side. Brush the edges with water. Fold the top and bottom over and then fold in the sides to form a sealed roll.

Just before serving, heat the oil for frying in a large skillet or wok until nearly smoking. Deep-fry the rolls, in batches, for 2–3 minutes, or until golden brown. Drain on paper towels while cooking the remainder. Serve with sweet chili dipping sauce.

# chicken satay

very easy

serves 8 as a starter

10 minutes + 1 hour to marinate

10 minutes

## ingredients

2 lb/900 g chicken breast meat, cut into ¼-inch/5-mm thick, 1-inch/2.5-cm wide strips

### MARINADE

2 tbsp corn oil

2 tbsp soy sauce

2 tsp tamarind paste

1 lemongrass stalk (tender inner part only), chopped coarsely

2 garlic cloves, crushed

1 tsp ground cumin

1 tsp ground coriander

1 tbsp lime juice

1 tsp soft light brown sugar

### PEANUT SAUCE

2 tbsp smooth peanut butter

scant 1 cup coconut cream

2 tsp red Thai curry paste

1 tbsp fish sauce

1 tbsp soft light brown sugar

Thread the chicken onto bamboo skewers.

To make the marinade, place the oil, soy sauce, tamarind paste, lemongrass, garlic, cumin, coriander, lime juice, and sugar in a food processor and blend to make a paste. Transfer to a bowl.

Add the chicken to the marinade and toss to coat. Cover with plastic wrap and refrigerate for at least 1 hour to marinate.

To make the peanut sauce, put the peanut butter, coconut cream, red Thai curry paste, fish sauce, and sugar in a pan. Heat gently, stirring, to form a smooth sauce.

Grill the chicken on a barbecue or under a broiler for 3–5 minutes on each side, or until the chicken is cooked through. Reheat the sauce, adding a little hot water if necessary, and serve with the chicken satays.

# thai pork appetizer

very easy   serves 6

20 minutes   20 minutes

## ingredients

4 garlic cloves, chopped finely
2 fresh red chilies, seeded and
   chopped finely
1 tbsp chopped cilantro root
1 tbsp grated fresh gingerroot
3 tbsp corn oil
1 tbsp hot water
1 lb 2 oz/500 g lean ground pork
2 fresh kaffir lime leaves, shredded finely

2 tbsp fish sauce
1 tsp soft light brown sugar
2 tbsp coarsely chopped fresh cilantro

TO GARNISH
fresh cilantro leaves
thin strips of red chili

crisp lettuce cups, to serve

Place the garlic, chilies, cilantro root, gingerroot, oil, and water in a blender, then blend until smooth. Transfer to a wok or skillet.

Heat and stir the paste for 4 minutes over a medium heat, then increase the heat and add the ground pork. Stir-fry for 3 minutes, or until colored.

Add the lime leaves, fish sauce, sugar, and chopped cilantro. Continue to cook, stirring, until the pork is dry.

Serve the pork in lettuce cups, garnished with cilantro leaves and strips of chili.

# hot chili relish with crudités

extremely easy

serves 4

10 minutes    15 minutes

**RELISH**

8–10 large red chilies, seeded
  and chopped finely
6 garlic cloves, chopped finely
½ cup water
½ tsp salt
2 tsp sugar
juice of 1 lime
1 tbsp fish sauce
1 tbsp vegetable oil

**SERVING SUGGESTIONS**

carrot sticks
radishes
cucumber batons
baby corn

Put all the relish ingredients in a pan and bring to a boil. Cover and simmer for 10 minutes.

Transfer the mixture to a food processor and blend until smooth.

Transfer the relish to a bowl and serve with vegetables.

# thai omelet

very easy

serves 2

15 minutes

30–35 minutes

### ingredients

6 eggs
salt and pepper
1 tbsp butter
1 tbsp oil

**FILLING**
1 tbsp oil
1 small onion, chopped finely
1 garlic clove, crushed
1 cup ground pork

1 cup green peas
2 tomatoes, peeled, seeded,
    and cut into ½-inch/1-cm dice
2 tsp fish sauce
1 tsp sugar
2 tsp lime juice
1 tbsp tomato ketchup
4 scallions, chopped finely

salad, to serve

To make the filling, first heat the oil in a skillet. Add the onion and garlic and cook gently for 10 minutes, or until soft. Add the pork and cook, stirring, for 5 minutes, or until colored.

Add the peas, tomatoes, fish sauce, sugar, lime juice, tomato ketchup, and scallions. Cook, stirring, for 10 minutes, adding a little water if the mixture is too dry.

In a bowl, whisk 3 of the eggs and season with salt and pepper.

Heat half the butter and oil in an omelet pan. Add the eggs and cook for 2–3 minutes, pulling in the edges with a fork and letting any egg run to the bottom of the pan.

When almost set, place half the filling mixture on 1 half of the omelet. Fold over and transfer to a plate. Keep warm while making the second omelet. Serve with salad.

Thailand has a long coastline and a large number of the people live near the sea. Thai cuisine has always made use of the abundance of fish and shellfish, and it includes many delicious recipes for fish, shrimp, crabs, and mussels. Traditional Thai dishes such as Fish Cakes and Shrimp & Pineapple Curry are quick and easy to make using ready-made Thai fish sauce, while Tiger Shrimp Skewers and Spiced Steamed Fish will liven up any dinner table.

fish & seafood

# thai fish cakes

very easy    serves 4

15 minutes    30 minutes
+ 30 minutes
to chill

## ingredients

1 lb 2 oz/500 g skinless, boneless
   cod fillet, cut into chunks
1 tbsp red curry paste
1 egg, beaten
1 tsp brown sugar
1 tsp salt
1 tbsp cornstarch
½ cup green beans, chopped finely
1 tbsp chopped fresh cilantro

4 tbsp oil, for frying
lime wedges, to garnish

SERVING SUGGESTIONS
salad
green beans
broccoli
snow peas

Put the cod into in a food processor and chop coarsely. Add the curry paste, egg, sugar, salt, and cornstarch. Blend well.

Stir in the green beans and cilantro.

Transfer to a bowl and cover with plastic wrap, then chill in the refrigerator for 30 minutes. Roll the mixture into 12 balls, then flatten each ball into a 2-inch/5-cm cake.

Heat the oil in a skillet over a medium heat and cook the cakes in batches for about 3 minutes on each side, or until golden brown and cooked through. Keep the cooked fish cakes warm in a low oven while cooking the remainder.

Garnish with the lime wedges and serve with salad or stir-fried green vegetables such as beans, snow peas, or broccoli.

# shrimp & pineapple curry

extremely
easy

serves 4

10 minutes

10–15
minutes

## ingredients

2 cups coconut cream
½ fresh pineapple, peeled and chopped
2 tbsp Thai red curry paste
2 tbsp fish sauce
2 tsp sugar

12 oz/350 g raw tiger shrimp, shelled
  and deveined

2 tbsp chopped fresh cilantro, to decorate

steamed jasmine rice, to serve

Place the coconut cream, pineapple, curry paste, fish sauce, and sugar in a skillet. Heat gently over a medium heat until almost boiling. Add the shrimp and cilantro and simmer gently for 3 minutes, or until the shrimp are cooked.

Serve with steamed jasmine rice.

# thai fish curry

easy     serves 4

20 minutes    20 minutes

## ingredients

4 shallots, chopped coarsely
2-inch/5-cm piece fresh gingerroot, peeled
   and sliced finely
2-inch/5-cm piece fresh lemongrass,
   outer leaves discarded
2-inch/5-cm piece fresh galangal, peeled
   and chopped finely
3 red chilies, seeded and chopped coarsely
1 tbsp ground almonds
½ tsp turmeric

½ tsp salt
1¾ cups coconut cream
4 fish steaks, eg cod, halibut

1 red chili, cut into thin strips, to garnish

**TO SERVE**
cooked white rice
salad

Place the shallots, gingerroot, lemongrass, galangal, chilies, ground almonds, turmeric, and salt in a blender. Add 6 tablespoons of the coconut cream. Blend to a smooth paste.

Pour the paste into a large skillet. Bring to a boil and cook, stirring, for 4 minutes. Add the remaining coconut milk and bring back to a boil.

Place the fish steaks in the skillet and simmer for 10 minutes, turning once, until the fish is cooked and flakes when tested with a fork. If the sauce is too thin, transfer the fish to a heated serving dish and boil the sauce to reduce to the desired consistency. Garnish with red chili and serve with rice and a salad of your choice.

# tiger shrimp skewers

easy    serves 4

15 minutes    5 minutes
+ 1 hour to
marinate

**MARINADE**
3 garlic cloves, crushed
2 shallots, chopped finely
1-inch/2.5-cm piece fresh gingerroot,
    peeled and grated finely
1 lemongrass stalk, chopped finely
1 fresh red chili, chopped finely
pinch of salt
1 tbsp lime juice

1 tbsp soy sauce
2 tbsp rice wine or dry sherry
12 raw tiger shrimp, in shells

**TO GARNISH**
cilantro sprigs
lime wedges

3 oranges, to serve

To make the marinade, place the garlic, shallots, gingerroot, lemongrass, chili, salt, lime juice, soy sauce, and rice wine or sherry in a blender and blend until smooth. Transfer to a shallow bowl.

Using a small knife, or scissors, split the shrimp shells down the back, but leave attached. Devein if necessary. Add to the marinade. Cover with plastic wrap and place in the refrigerator to marinate for 30 minutes to 1 hour.

Thread each shrimp onto a bamboo skewer, inserting the skewer at the tail and coming out at the head end until the pointed end extends at least 3 inches/7 cm beyond the shrimp.

Broil for 2 minutes on each side, or until the shrimp are pink and cooked through. Garnish with the cilantro sprigs and lime wedges. Stick the skewers in the oranges, to serve.

# spiced steamed fish

very easy    serves 4–6

10 minutes   20–25
minutes

## ingredients

1-inch/2.5-cm piece gingerroot,
    grated finely
1 lemongrass stalk (base only),
    sliced thinly
6 fresh red chilies, seeded and
    chopped coarsely
1 small red onion, chopped finely
1 tbsp fish sauce

2 lb/900 g whole fish (eg sea bass,
    red snapper, trout, tilapia), cleaned
2 kaffir lime leaves, sliced thinly
2 sprigs fresh basil leaves

**TO SERVE**
cooked rice
cucumber batons

Place the gingerroot, lemongrass, chilies, onion, and fish sauce in a blender.
Chop coarsely to a rough paste, adding a little water, if necessary.

Cut 3–4 deep slits crosswise on each side of the fish. Spread over the spice paste,
rubbing it well into the slits.

Place the fish in a dish deep enough to hold the liquid that collects during
steaming. Sprinkle over the lime leaves and basil.

Set up a steamer or put a rack into a wok or deep skillet. Bring about 2 inches/5 cm
of water to a boil in the steamer or wok. Put the dish of fish into the steamer
or onto the rack. Reduce the heat to a simmer. Cover tightly and steam the fish
for 15–20 minutes, or until the fish is cooked through. Serve with rice and
cucumber batons.

# fragrant mussels

easy     serves 2–3

10 minutes    15–20 minutes

## ingredients

2 lb 4 oz/1 kg mussels, cleaned

2 tbsp water

1 lemongrass stalk, bruised

2 garlic cloves, crushed

3 fresh or dried kaffir lime leaves, chopped coarsely

scant 1 cup coconut cream

2 tbsp chopped fresh cilantro

salt and pepper

warm, crusty bread, to serve

Clean the mussels by scrubbing the shells and pulling out any beards that are attached. Rinse well, discarding any that are broken or remain open when tapped.

Put the water, lemongrass, garlic, and lime leaves in a large pan. Bring to a boil. Add the mussels, then cover and cook for 5–6 minutes, or until they have opened. Discard any that stay closed. Transfer the mussels to a heated serving dish, then cover and keep warm in a low oven.

Boil the cooking liquid hard until reduced by half, then stir in the coconut cream. Boil to reduce and thicken slightly. Add the cilantro and season to taste.

Pour over the mussels and serve with warm, crusty bread.

Chicken and duck are widely used in Thai cooking. Many families keep their own chickens and ducks and, because they are free range, they tend to be smaller and tougher than the ones we buy. Most recipes, such as the traditional Green Chicken Curry, are quickly prepared in a wok. Pork is the most popular meat, but beef is also used in classical recipes such as Thai Beef Curry. Lamb is becoming more popular and, in most of the recipes, the meat used can be varied to suit your taste. Also in this section are main course salads made with beef or duck.

meat & poultry

# grilled beef salad

very easy    serves 4

10 minutes    5–10
+ 20 minutes  minutes
to soak
mushrooms

## ingredients

DRESSING

2 tbsp sesame oil

2 tbsp fish sauce

2 tbsp sweet sherry

2 tbsp oyster sauce

1 tbsp lime juice

1 fresh red chili, seeded and chopped finely

scant ⅔ cup dried oyster mushrooms

1 lb 5 oz/600 g rump steak

1 red bell pepper, seeded and sliced thinly

generous ¼ cup roasted cashew nuts

red and green lettuce leaves, to serve

mint leaves, to garnish

To make the dressing, place the sesame oil, fish sauce, sherry, oyster sauce, lime juice, and chili in a bowl and whisk to combine.

Place the mushrooms in a bowl, then cover with boiling water and let stand for 20 minutes. Drain and cut into thin slices.

Grill the beef, either on a ridged iron grill pan or under the broiler, turning once, for 5 minutes, or until browned on both sides and rare in the middle, or cook longer if desired.

Slice the steak into thin strips and place in a bowl with the mushrooms, bell pepper, and nuts. Add the dressing and toss together.

Arrange the lettuce on a serving platter and place the beef mixture on top. Garnish with mint and serve at room temperature.

# thai beef curry

easy    serves 4

15 minutes    1½–2 hours

## ingredients

3 tbsp corn oil
1 lb 12 oz/800 g braising steak, cubed
2 onions, sliced thinly
2 tbsp Thai red curry paste
1 tbsp tamarind paste or lime juice
2 tbsp fish sauce
3¾ cups coconut milk

2 tsp sugar
6 cardamom pods, crushed
1 small pineapple, peeled and chopped

**TO SERVE**
cooked rice
shrimp chips

Heat the oil in a flameproof casserole. Brown the beef in batches and set aside.

Add the onions to the oil and cook for 5 minutes, then set aside with the beef. Add the curry paste and cook gently for 1 minute, stirring constantly.

Stir in the tamarind paste, fish sauce, coconut milk, and sugar. Bring to a boil, then reduce the heat and return the beef and onions to the casserole with the cardamom.

Simmer gently, uncovered, for 1–1½ hours, or until the meat is tender. Stir from time to time and if it is becoming dry, cover with a lid.

Add the pineapple and cook for 5 more minutes. The curry should be quite dry, but add a little water if necessary.

Serve with rice and shrimp chips.

# pork steaks with lemongrass

extremely easy

serves 4

5 minutes
+ 1 hour to
marinate

10 minutes

MARINADE

2 garlic cloves, crushed

½ tsp pepper

1 tbsp sugar

2 tbsp fish sauce

2 tbsp soy sauce

1 tbsp sesame oil

1 tbsp lime juice

2 lemongrass stalks, outer leaves removed,
    chopped finely

4 scallions, chopped finely

2 tbsp coconut milk

4 pork steaks

lime wedges, to garnish

TO SERVE

salad

stir-fried vegetables

To make the marinade, place the garlic, pepper, sugar, fish sauce, soy sauce, sesame oil, lime juice, lemongrass, scallions, and coconut milk in a large shallow dish and mix well to combine.

Turn the pork steaks in the marinade, then cover the dish with plastic wrap and place in the refrigerator for 1 hour.

Broil the pork steaks under a preheated broiler or barbecue them over charcoal, for 5 minutes on each side, or until cooked through. Garnish with lime wedges and serve with salad or stir-fried vegetables.

# tamarind pork

very easy

serves 4

15 minutes

8–10 minutes

## ingredients

SPICE PASTE
4 shallots, chopped finely
2 garlic cloves, chopped finely
1-inch/2.5-cm piece fresh gingerroot,
  peeled and chopped finely
1 tsp ground coriander
2 fresh red chilies, seeded and
  chopped finely
½ tsp ground turmeric
6 blanched almonds, chopped finely

2 tbsp tamarind paste
2 tbsp hot water

2 tbsp corn oil
1 lb 5 oz/600 g lean pork,
  cut into thin strips
8 oz/225 g canned bamboo shoots,
  drained

cooked noodles, to serve

To make the spice paste, place the shallots, garlic, gingerroot, ground coriander, chilies, turmeric, almonds, tamarind paste, and water in a food processor and blend until smooth.

In a wok or skillet, heat the oil over a high heat. Add the pork and cook for 3 minutes, or until the meat is colored. Then add the spice paste and continue to cook for 2 or 3 more minutes.

Add the bamboo shoots and cook for 2 more minutes, or until the pork is cooked through. Serve with hot noodles.

# stir-fried lamb with mint

easy     serves 4

15 minutes    30 minutes
(food cooked
in batches)

## ingredients

2 tbsp corn oil

2 garlic cloves, sliced finely

2 fresh red chilies, seeded and
    cut into thin strips

1 onion, sliced thinly

1½ tbsp Madras curry powder

1 lb 2 oz/500 g lamb fillet,
    cut into thin strips

8 oz/225 g canned baby corn, drained

4 scallions, chopped finely

generous ⅓ cup fresh mint leaves,
    shredded coarsely

1 tbsp fish sauce

cooked rice, to serve

Heat half the oil in a wok or skillet. Add the garlic and chili and cook until soft. Remove and set aside. Add the onion and cook for 5 minutes, or until soft. Remove and set aside.

Heat the remaining oil in the wok, add the curry powder and cook for 1 minute. Add the lamb, in batches if necessary, and cook for 5–8 minutes, or until cooked through and tender.

Return the onion to the wok with the baby sweetcorn, scallions, mint, and fish sauce. Cook until heated through. Scatter the garlic and chili over and serve with rice.

# stir-fried chicken with thai basil

very easy    serves 4

15 minutes    15 minutes

2 tbsp corn oil

4 garlic cloves, crushed

4 scallions, chopped finely

4 green chilies, seeded and chopped finely

1 green bell pepper, seeded and
 sliced thinly

1 lb 5 oz/600 g skinless, boneless chicken
 breast fillets, cut into thin strips

generous ⅓ cup fresh Thai basil leaves,
 chopped coarsely

2 tbsp fish sauce

basil leaves, to garnish

cooked rice, to serve

Heat the oil in a wok. Add the garlic and scallions and cook for 1–2 minutes,
or until soft.

Add the chili and green bell pepper and cook for 2 minutes.

Add the chicken and cook until browned. Stir in the basil and fish sauce, and cook
for a few more minutes, or until the chicken is cooked through. Garnish with basil
leaves and serve with rice.

# quick green chicken curry

extremely easy    serves 4

5 minutes    10 minutes

## ingredients

1 tbsp corn oil

6 scallions, sliced

1 lb 5oz/600 g skinless, boneless chicken
  breast, cut into cubes

scant 1 cup coconut cream

3 tbsp green Thai curry paste

3 tbsp chopped fresh cilantro

cooked noodles or rice, to serve

Heat the oil in a large skillet. Add the scallions and the chicken and cook, stirring, for 3–4 minutes, or until the chicken is browned.

Stir in the coconut cream and curry paste and cook for another 5 minutes, or until the chicken is cooked through. Add a little water or bouillon if the sauce becomes too thick.

Stir in the chopped cilantro and serve with rice or noodles.

# chicken with lemongrass & chili

very easy    serves 4

10 minutes   50 minutes

## ingredients

2 tbsp corn oil

4 garlic cloves, sliced thinly

1 onion, sliced thinly

2 lemongrass stalks, outer part removed, chopped very finely

2 red chilies, seeded and chopped finely

8 chicken thighs

3 tbsp fish sauce

1 tbsp light brown sugar

1 cup chicken bouillon

Heat the oil in a large skillet. Add the garlic and onion and cook gently for 5–10 minutes, or until soft.

Add the lemongrass and chili and cook for 2 minutes. Add the chicken and cook for 5 minutes, or until browned all over.

Add the fish sauce, sugar, and bouillon. Bring to a boil, then reduce the heat and simmer, covered, for 30 minutes, or until the chicken is cooked through and tender. Stir occasionally and add water, if necessary. Serve immediately.

# peanut-crusted chicken
# with dipping sauce

easy    serves 6

20 minutes    35 minutes

## ingredients

2 garlic cloves, crushed

1-inch/2.5-cm piece fresh gingerroot,
   peeled and grated finely

1 lemongrass stalk, outer leaves removed,
   chopped finely

2 tbsp chopped fresh cilantro leaves

scant 1⅓ cups salted peanuts

¾ cup all-purpose flour

2 eggs

4 tbsp milk

12 chicken drumsticks, skin removed

### DIPPING SAUCE

1 fresh red chili, seeded and chopped finely

2 garlic cloves, crushed

½ cup white wine vinegar

2 tbsp dark brown sugar

Preheat the oven to 425°F/220°C. Place the garlic, gingerroot, lemongrass, cilantro leaves, peanuts, and 2 tablespoons of the flour in a food processor and blend until finely ground. Transfer to a shallow dish.

In a bowl, beat together the eggs and milk. Spread the remaining flour on a plate. Dip the drumsticks into the flour, then into the egg mixture and finally into the peanut mixture. Arrange them in an oiled roasting pan. Bake in the oven for 15 minutes, then turn them and cook for another 15 minutes. Pour off any excess oil and cook the drumsticks for 5 more minutes, or until very crisp.

To make the sauce, grind the chili and garlic to a paste using a mortar and pestle. Put the vinegar and sugar in a pan. Heat gently until the sugar dissolves. Bring to a boil and simmer for 2 minutes. Stir in the chili/garlic paste. Transfer to a bowl. Drain the drumsticks on paper towels and serve with the sauce.

# roast duck salad

very easy  serves 4

20 minutes

20–30 minutes

2 duck breasts
2 Boston lettuces, shredded
1 cup beansprouts
1 yellow bell pepper, seeded and
  cut into thin strips
½ cucumber, seeded and
  cut into short thin sticks

**TO GARNISH**
2 tsp shredded lime zest
2 tbsp shredded coconut, toasted

**DRESSING**
juice of 2 limes
3 tbsp fish sauce
1 tbsp soft brown sugar
2 tsp sweet chili sauce
1-inch/2.5-cm piece fresh gingerroot,
  grated finely
3 tbsp chopped fresh mint
3 tbsp chopped fresh basil

Preheat the oven to 400°F/200°C. Place the duck breasts on a rack set over a roasting pan and roast in the oven for 20–30 minutes, or until cooked as desired and the skin is crisp. Remove from the oven and set aside to cool.

In a large bowl, combine the lettuce, beansprouts, bell pepper, and cucumber. Cut the cooled duck into strips and add to the salad. Mix well.

In a bowl, whisk together the lime juice, fish sauce, sugar, chili sauce, gingerroot, mint, and basil. Add the dressing to the salad and toss well.

Turn the salad out onto a serving platter and garnish with the lime zest and shredded coconut before serving.

The vegetable dishes in this section, such as Stir-fried Green Vegetables, can be served as an accompaniment to the main course, or you could serve one or two of the dishes with noodles or rice as a light lunch or supper. If you omit the fish sauce, they are suitable for vegetarians. Rice is the staple food of Thailand, and plain cooked fragrant rice is served at every meal. Spicy Fried Rice is a good accompaniment to a plain main course or can be served as a dish in its own right. Noodles can be combined with a wide variety of different ingredients and are equally good served hot or cold.

# vegetables, salads, noodles & rice

# stir-fried green vegetables

extremely easy serves 4

15 minutes 10 minutes

2 tbsp corn oil
3 garlic cloves, sliced thinly
1-inch/2.5-cm piece fresh gingerroot,
   sliced thinly
6 oz/175 g baby spinach leaves, washed
   and drained
1 small head broccoli, cut into small florets
4 oz/115 g green beans, trimmed
   and halved

1 cup snow peas, trimmed and halved
pepper
1 tbsp fish sauce
1 tbsp oyster sauce
1 tsp sugar
4 scallions, chopped diagonally

Heat the oil in a wok. Cook the garlic and ginger for 1 minute, then add the spinach, broccoli, and beans and cook for 2 minutes.

Add the snow peas and cook all the vegetables over a high heat, for 2 minutes.

Add the pepper, fish sauce, oyster sauce, sugar, and scallions and continue to cook for another 2 minutes.

Transfer to a heated serving plate and serve at once.

# vegetable & coconut curry

easy

serves 4

20 minutes

40–50 minutes

**ingredients**

1 onion, chopped coarsely
3 garlic cloves, sliced thinly
1-inch/2.5-cm piece fresh gingerroot, sliced thinly
2 fresh green chilies, seeded and chopped finely
1 tbsp corn oil
1 tsp ground turmeric
1 tsp ground coriander

1 tsp ground cumin
2 lb 4 oz/1 kg mixed vegetables (eg, cauliflower, zucchini, potatoes, carrots, green beans), cut into chunks
7 oz/200 g creamed coconut
2½ cups boiling water
salt and pepper

cooked rice, to serve

Put the onion, garlic, gingerroot, and chilies in a food processor and blend until almost smooth.

Heat the oil in a large pan, then add the onion mixture and cook gently for 5 minutes, stirring constantly.

Add the turmeric, coriander, and cumin and cook for 3–4 minutes, stirring. Add the vegetables and stir to coat in the spice paste.

In a pitcher, mix together the creamed coconut and boiling water and stir until dissolved. Add this coconut milk to the vegetables, then cover and simmer for 30–40 minutes, or until the vegetables are tender.

Season with salt and pepper, and serve with rice.

# thai salad with peanut dressing

easy     serves 4

15 minutes    10 minutes

2¼ cups white cabbage, shredded
4 carrots, cut into short thin sticks
4 celery stalks, cut into short thin sticks
2¼ cups bean sprouts
½ cucumber, cut into short thin sticks

**PEANUT SAUCE**
2 tbsp smooth peanut butter
scant 1 cup coconut cream
2 tsp red Thai curry paste
1 tbsp fish sauce
1 tbsp soft brown sugar

**TO GARNISH**
fried onion
sliced green chili

In a steamer set above a pan of boiling water, steam the cabbage, carrots, and celery for 3–4 minutes, or until just tender. Let cool.

Arrange the bean sprouts on a large shallow serving dish. Arrange the cabbage, carrots, celery, and cucumber on top.

To make the sauce, place the peanut butter, coconut cream, red Thai curry paste, fish sauce, and sugar in a pan. Heat gently, stirring, adding a little hot water, if necessary, to make a coating sauce. Spoon a little of the sauce over the vegetables and then garnish with fried onions and sliced chili. Serve the rest of the sauce separately.

# green papaya salad

very easy    serves 4–6

15 minutes   3 minutes

## ingredients

2 cups snow peas
2 unripe papayas

### DRESSING
2 garlic cloves, crushed
2 fresh red chilies, seeded and
    chopped finely
1 tsp sugar
2 tbsp soy sauce
juice of 1 lime

### TO GARNISH
12 cherry tomatoes, halved
2 tbsp chopped peanuts

½ head Napa cabbage, to serve

Place the snow peas in a pan of boiling salted water. Bring back to a boil and cook for 2 minutes. Drain into a strainer, then refresh with cold water. Cut into short thin sticks and place in a bowl.

Peel the papayas and remove the seeds, then grate into the bowl with the snow peas. Chill until ready to serve.

In a bowl, mix together the garlic, chilies, sugar, soy sauce, and lime juice. Pour over the papaya salad and mix well.

Arrange the Napa cabbage in a large serving bowl. Put the salad on top and garnish with the halved tomatoes and chopped peanuts before serving.

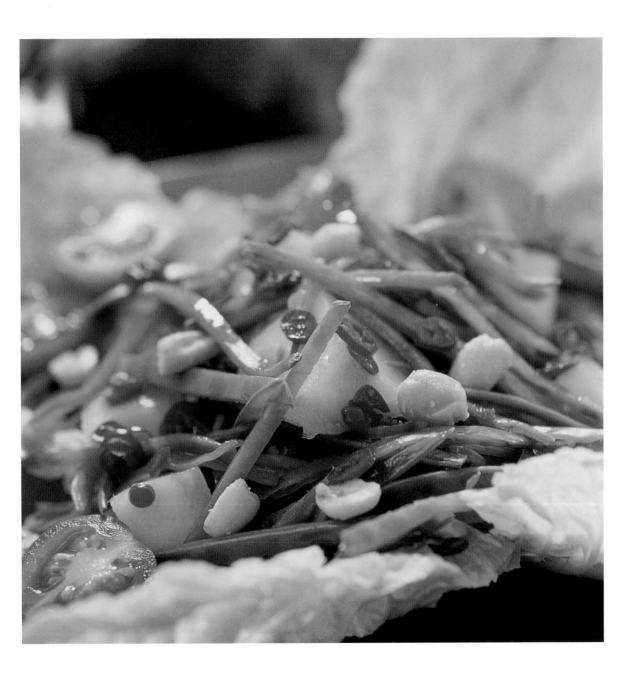

# pineapple & cucumber salad

very easy  serves 4

20 minutes  none

## ingredients

1 cucumber

1 small fresh pineapple

1 red onion, sliced thinly

1 bunch watercress

DRESSING

3 tbsp lemon juice

2 tbsp soy sauce

1 tsp sugar

1 tsp chili sauce

2 tbsp chopped fresh mint

Peel the cucumber and cut into fourths lengthwise. Scoop out the seeds with a teaspoon and cut each fourth into ½-inch/1-cm pieces. Place in a bowl.

Peel the pineapple and cut into fourths, lengthwise. Remove the core. Cut each fourth in half lengthwise and cut into ½-inch/1-cm pieces and add to the cucumber. Add the onion and watercress and mix.

To make the dressing, place the lemon juice, soy sauce, sugar, chili sauce, and mint in a bowl and whisk together.

Pour the dressing over the salad and toss together. Transfer to a large serving platter and serve at once.

# noodles with shrimp & green bell peppers

very easy    serves 4

10 minutes   10 minutes

## ingredients

9 oz/250 g rice noodles
1 tbsp corn oil
2 garlic cloves, crushed
1 fresh red chili, seeded and
   sliced thinly
1 green bell pepper, seeded and
   sliced thinly

6 scallions, chopped coarsely
2 tsp cornstarch
2 tbsp oyster sauce
1 tbsp fish sauce
1 tsp sugar
1 cup chicken bouillon
9 oz/250 g small cooked shrimp, shelled

Prepare the noodles as directed on the package. Drain, then refresh under cold water and drain again.

Heat the oil in a wok. Add the garlic, chili, bell pepper, and scallions. Cook for 1 minute, then remove from the wok to a plate and set aside.

Blend the cornstarch with a little water and add to the wok with the oyster sauce, fish sauce, sugar, and bouillon. Stir over a medium heat until the mixture boils and thickens.

Return the bell pepper and scallion mixture to the wok with the shrimp and the noodles. Cook, stirring, for 2 minutes, or until heated through. Transfer to a heated serving bowl and serve.

# fried egg noodles

extremely easy

serves 4

10 minutes

10 minutes

## ingredients

9 oz/250 g fine egg noodles
2 tbsp corn oil
2 garlic cloves, crushed
1 tbsp fish sauce
3 tbsp lime juice
1 tsp sugar
2 eggs, beaten lightly

4 oz/115 g cooked shrimp, shelled
1 cup bean sprouts
6 scallions, sliced finely

TO GARNISH
2 tbsp finely chopped roasted peanuts
handful of cilantro leaves

Prepare the noodles as directed on the package. Drain, then rinse with cold water and drain again. Set aside.

Heat the oil in a wok. Add the garlic and cook, stirring, for 1 minute, or until lightly browned but not burned. Stir in the fish sauce, lime juice, and sugar and stir until the sugar has dissolved.

Quickly stir in the eggs and cook for a few seconds. Stir in the noodles to coat with the garlic and eggs. Add the shrimp, bean sprouts, and half the scallions.

When everything is heated through, transfer the mixture to a warmed serving dish. Sprinkle the remaining scallions on top and serve, garnished with peanuts, and cilantro leaves.

# hot & sour noodle salad

extremely easy

serves 4

5 minutes

5 minutes

## ingredients

12 oz/350 g rice vermicelli
4 tbsp sesame oil
3 tbsp soy sauce
juice of 2 limes

1 tsp sugar
4 scallions, sliced finely
1–2 tsp hot chili sauce
2 tbsp chopped fresh cilantro

Prepare the vermicelli as directed on the package. Drain, then place in a bowl and toss with half the sesame oil.

In a bowl, mix together the remaining oil, the soy sauce, lime juice, sugar, scallions, and chili sauce. Stir into the noodles.

Stir in the cilantro and serve.

# spicy fried rice

easy     serves 4–6

15 minutes   25 minutes
+ 20 minutes
to soak
mushrooms

## ingredients

1¼ cups long-grain rice
scant ½ cup dried mushrooms
2 tbsp corn oil
2 eggs, beaten lightly
2 garlic cloves, chopped finely
1 fresh red chili, seeded and chopped finely
½-inch/1-cm piece fresh gingerroot,
    grated finely

2 tbsp soy sauce
1 tsp sugar
2 tsp fish sauce
6 scallions, chopped finely
1 lb/450 g cooked, shelled small shrimp
14 oz/400 g canned baby corn, drained
    and cut in half

Place the rice in a strainer and rinse under cold water. Drain thoroughly. Add the rice to a large pan of boiling salted water, then bring back to a boil and cook for about 10 minutes, or until tender. Drain, rinse under cold water, and drain again.

Place the mushrooms in a bowl, cover with warm water, and let stand for 20 minutes. Drain and cut into slices.

Heat half the oil in a wok. Add the eggs. Stir the uncooked egg to the outside edge of the wok. Cook until firm. Remove the omelet, roll up firmly, and cut into strips.

Heat the remaining oil in the wok, then add the garlic, chili, and gingerroot and cook for 1 minute. Add the soy sauce, sugar, fish sauce, and scallions, stirring to dissolve the sugar. Stir in the reserved rice, shrimp, and corn, tossing to mix. Cook for 3–4 minutes, or until the rice is heated through. Turn into a warm serving bowl and serve at once.

Desserts other than fresh fruit are not usually served at a Thai meal, but are more likely to appear at banquets and festive occasions. The dishes in this section are delicious at any time, whether served after dinner or as a snack at another time of day. These desserts are all light, and most include fruit. Tropical Fruit in a Lemongrass Syrup is fragrant and refreshing at the end of a meal. Coconut milk or cream are widely used in the savory recipes in this book, but they also make creamy desserts such as Coconut & Ginger Ice Cream and Coconut Cream Custard.

desserts

# mango with sticky rice

very easy    serves 4

30 minutes   35 minutes
+ 30 minutes
to soak rice

## ingredients

generous 1 cup glutinous rice, soaked for
  30 minutes in cold water
1 cup coconut milk

2 tbsp superfine sugar
pinch of salt
2 large ripe mangoes

Drain the rice and rinse thoroughly. Place in a pan with the coconut milk, sugar, and salt. Bring to a boil and simmer, stirring occasionally, until the rice has absorbed all the coconut milk and is very soft.

Transfer the rice to a steamer set over a pan of simmering water. Cover and steam for 15 minutes. Let cool a little. Spread the rice out on a cookie sheet lined with foil, then roll the rice flat with a wet rolling pin. Cut into diamond shapes.

Peel the mangoes and cut the flesh into cubes. Arrange the rice diamonds and mango cubes on individual plates or in ramekins and serve.

# coconut cream custard

extremely easy  serves 4

10 minutes  20–30 minutes

## ingredients

4 large eggs
generous ½ cup superfine sugar
scant 1 cup coconut cream
1 tbsp rosewater

fresh fruit, to serve

Preheat the oven to 350°F/180°C.

In a bowl, beat together the eggs, sugar, coconut cream, and rosewater and stir until the sugar is dissolved.

Divide the custard into four ramekins. Place in a roasting pan and pour in boiling water to come halfway up the sides of the ramekins. Bake in the oven for 20–30 minutes, or until set. Remove from the tin and let cool.

To turn out, run a sharp knife round the edge of each custard and turn out onto a serving dish. Serve with fresh fruit.

# tropical fruit in lemongrass syrup

easy    serves 4

15 minutes   15 minutes
+ 12 hours
to chill

### ingredients

**LEMONGRASS SYRUP**
1½ cups superfine sugar
⅔ cup water
2 lemongrass stalks, bruised
2 kaffir lime leaves
juice of 1 lime

1 honeydew melon
1 small pineapple
1 papaya
14 oz/400 g litchis, pitted
3 passion fruit

**DECORATION**
small handful of fresh mint leaves

To make the syrup, place the sugar, water, lemongrass, lime leaves, and lime juice in a pan. Heat gently until the sugar has dissolved. Bring to a boil and boil, uncovered, for 5 minutes. Set aside overnight.

Cut the melon in half, then remove the seeds and scoop out the flesh with a melon baller. Place in a bowl. Peel the pineapple, then cut into fourths lengthwise and remove the core. Cut into cubes and add to the melon. Peel the papaya, then remove the seeds and cut the flesh into cubes and add to the other fruit.

Add the litchis. Cut the passion fruit in half and scoop the pulp and seeds into the bowl of fruit. Stir to combine, then transfer to a serving bowl. Remove the lemongrass and lime leaves from the syrup and pour over the fruit. Decorate with mint leaves and serve.

# thai crêpes with papaya & passion fruit

easy     serves 4

15 minutes    20 minutes

### ingredients

2 eggs
½ cup coconut milk
¾ cup milk
1 cup all-purpose flour
½ tsp salt
1 tbsp superfine sugar
1 tbsp butter, melted
oil, for frying
sifted confectioners' sugar, for dusting

**FILLING**
2 papaya
3 passion fruit
juice of 1 lime
2 tbsp confectioners' sugar

In a bowl, whisk together the eggs, coconut milk, and milk. Sift the flour and salt into a large bowl. Stir in the sugar. Make a well in the middle of the flour and gradually beat in the egg mixture to form a smooth batter. Stir in the melted butter.

Heat an 8–9-inch/20–22-cm nonstick skillet and brush with oil. Pour in enough batter to coat the bottom of the skillet. Tip the skillet as you pour it in, so the bottom is evenly coated. Cook until browned on the underside and set on top, then turn the crêpe over and cook the other side. Place on a plate, then cover with foil and keep warm while making the remaining crêpes.

Peel the papaya and halve, then scoop out the seeds, reserving a few. Cut into chunks and place in a bowl. Cut the passion fruit in half. Scoop the seeds and pulp into the bowl. Stir in the lime juice and confectioners' sugar. Put a little filling on one fourth of each crêpe. Fold in half and then into fourths. Dust with sifted confectioners' sugar. Scatter on the reserved papaya seeds and serve.

# thai bananas

extremely
easy

serves 6

10 minutes

10 minutes

## ingredients

1½ cups coconut milk

2 tbsp granulated sugar

½ tsp salt

6 slightly underripe bananas, peeled and
   cut into 2-inch/5-cm lengths

1 tbsp toasted sesame seeds,
   to decorate

Place the coconut milk, sugar, and salt in a pan and heat gently until the sugar
is dissolved. Add the banana pieces and cook gently for 5 minutes, or until the
bananas are soft but not mushy.

Divide the mixture between 6 small bowls. Scatter the sesame seeds over
and serve.

# coconut & ginger ice cream

very easy    1¾ pints/
1 liter

20 minutes    10 minutes
+ 6–8 hours
to freeze

## ingredients

1¾ cups coconut milk
1 cup whipping cream
4 egg yolks
5 tbsp superfine sugar
4 tbsp syrup from the preserved ginger
6 pieces preserved ginger, drained and
   finely chopped
2 tbsp lime juice

**TO SERVE**
litchis
ginger syrup

Place the coconut milk and cream in a medium pan. Heat gently until just beginning to simmer. Remove from the heat.

In a large bowl, beat together the egg yolks, sugar, and ginger syrup until pale and creamy. Slowly pour in the hot milk mixture, while stirring. Return to the pan and heat gently, stirring constantly, until the mixture thickens and coats the back of a spoon. Remove from the heat and let cool. Stir in the ginger and lime juice.

Transfer the mixture to a freezerproof container. Cover and freeze for 2–3 hours, or until just frozen. Spoon into a bowl and mash with a fork or whisk to break down any ice crystals. Return the mixture to the container and freeze for 2 more hours. Mash once more, then freeze for 2–3 hours, or until firm. Remove from the freezer to the refrigerator 20–30 minutes before serving. Serve with litchis and a little ginger syrup drizzled over.

# easy mango ice cream

very easy

1¾ pints/
1 liter

10 minutes
+ 6–8 hours
to freeze

## ingredients

2½ cups ready-made traditional custard

⅔ cup whipping cream, whipped lightly

flesh of 2 ripe mangoes, puréed

confectioners' sugar, to taste

passion fruit pulp, to serve

In a large bowl, mix together the custard, cream, and mango pulp.

Taste for sweetness and, if necessary, add confectioners' sugar to taste, remembering that, when frozen, the mixture will taste less sweet.

Transfer the mixture to a freezerproof container. Cover and freeze for 2–3 hours, or until just frozen. Spoon into a bowl and mash with a fork or whisk to break down any ice crystals. Return the mixture to the container and freeze for 2 more hours. Mash once more, then freeze for 2–3 hours, or until firm.

Transfer from the freezer to the refrigerator 20–30 minutes before serving. Serve with the passion fruit pulp.

# index